My Favorite Bear

Andrea Gabriel

My Favorite Bear

🐾 Whispering Coyote
A Charlesbridge Imprint

This book is dedicated with the utmost love and
admiration to my grandmother, Sally Haase—
one of my favorite mama bears.

A Whispering Coyote Book
Published by Charlesbridge
85 Main Street
Watertown, MA 02472
(617) 926-0329
www.charlesbridge.com

Library of Congress Cataloging-in-Publication Data

Gabriel, Andrea.
My favorite bear / written and illustrated by Andrea Gabriel.
p. cm.
"A Whispering Coyote book."
Summary: As Mama bear puts her child to bed, she shares a lullaby about
bears of the world.
ISBN 1-58089-038-5 (reinforced for library use)
[1. Bedtime--Fiction. 2. Mother and child — Fiction. 3. Bears — Fiction.
4. Stories in rhyme.] I. Title.
PZ8.3.G112 My 2003
[E] — dc21   2002002285

Printed in Korea
(hc) 10 9 8 7 6 5 4 3 2 1

Display type set in Jimbo and text type set in Garamond No. 3.
Color separations by Pacifica Communications
Printed and bound by Pacifica Communications

You're my little bear.

One day you'll be grown.

You'll meet other bears

when you travel from home.

There are bears who like swimming

and bears climbing high,

bears eating berries,

and bears in the sky.

Some bears eat fish.

Some like bamboo.

Some bears hunt by
the light of the moon.

There are shy bears,
sticky bears,

and bears feeling lazy,

white bears,

black bears,

and bears sniffing daisies.

I'm glad there are bears
of all shapes and all types.

But my favorite bear—
the one who's just right...

. . . is my own sleepy cub.

I love you.
Good night.

Bear Facts

American Black Bear (*Ursus americanus*) Despite its name, the American black bear can be found in a variety of colors: cinnamon, pale blue, white, or brown. Black bears live in forests throughout Canada, the United States, and northern Mexico.

Brown Bear (*Ursus arctos*) The brown bear can be recognized by its shoulder hump and long front claws. Populations of brown bears are found in mountain, tundra, and forested areas of North America, Asia, and Europe.

Polar Bear (*Ursus maritimus*) Many of these bears live most of their lives on the ice, rarely setting foot on land. Polar bears are excellent swimmers, with large paws that propel them through the water. These bears are found throughout the polar regions, and live mostly on a diet of seals.

Asiatic Black Bear (*Ursus thibetanus*) The Asiatic black bear is believed to be a close relative of the American black bear. Asiatic bears have large rounded ears and a V-shaped white patch on their chests. They live in the forests, hills, and mountains of Asia and eat fruit, honey, insects, and carrion.

Sloth Bear (*Melursus ursinus*) The sloth bear is found in the forests and grasslands in and around India. Adapted to a diet of termites and other insects, the sloth bear uses its flexible snout to "vacuum" up its dinner. These bears carry their cubs on their backs, and can be quite aggressive when startled.

Giant Panda (*Ailuropoda melanoleuca*) The giant panda may be the most famous of all endangered species. Only about 1,000 of these bears remain in the wild, living in several mountain areas of China. Pandas mainly eat plants, chiefly bamboo.

Sun Bear (*Helarctos malayanus*) The sun bear is the smallest species of bear, some weighing only 60 pounds when full grown. They are found in the tropical rainforests of Southeast Asia, and live mostly on a diet of plants, insects, and bees' nests.

Spectacled Bear (*Tremarctos ornatus*) The spectacled bear gets its name from the distinctive mask on its face. It is the only species of bear to live in South America. It spends a great deal of time in the trees, and will sometimes build a "nest" for sleeping.